To:

From:

Text © 1997 by Garborg's Heart 'n Home, Inc.

Published by Garborg's Heart 'n Home, Inc., P.O. Box 20132, Bloomington, MN 55420

ISBN 1-881830-60-8

Mother, I Love You!

Many women do noble things,
but you surpass them all.

PROVERBS 31:29 NIV

God bless my mother,
all that I am or ever hope
to be I owe to her.

ABRAHAM LINCOLN

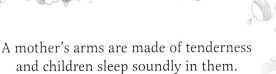

A mother's arms are made of tenderness
and children sleep soundly in them.

VICTOR HUGO

Mother is the name for God in the lips
and hearts of little children.

WILLIAM MAKEPEACE THACKERAY

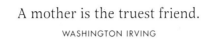

A mother is the truest friend.

WASHINGTON IRVING

The loveliest masterpiece of the heart of God
is the heart of a mother.

THÉRÈSE OF LISIEUX

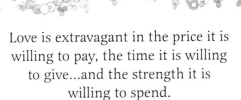

Love is extravagant in the price it is
willing to pay, the time it is willing
to give...and the strength it is
willing to spend.

JONI EARECKSON TADA

No one ever outgrows the need for a mother's love.

JANETTE OKE

Who is queen of baby land?
Mother kind and sweet,
And her love, born above,
Guides the little feet.

There's no love in the world
as precious as a mother's
And no mother quite
as precious as you.

Her children arise and call her blessed.

PROVERBS 31:28 NIV

A mother is...one who can take the
place of all others, but whose
place no one else can take.

G. MERMILLOD

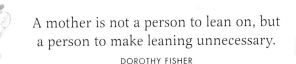

A mother is not a person to lean on, but
a person to make leaning unnecessary.

DOROTHY FISHER

A mother's heart is always with her children.

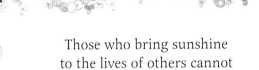

Those who bring sunshine
to the lives of others cannot
keep it from themselves.

JAMES M. BARRIE

No language can express the power and
beauty and heroism and majesty
of a mother's love.

E. H. CHAPIN

A mother's love endures through all.

WASHINGTON IRVING

Who ran to help me when I fell,
And would some pretty story tell,
Or kiss the place to make it well?
My Mother.

ANN TAYLOR

Nothing is so strong as gentleness and
nothing so gentle as real strength.

FRANCIS DE SALES

See how very much our heavenly Father loves us,
for he allows us to be called his children—
think of it—and we really *are!*

1 JOHN 3:1 TLB

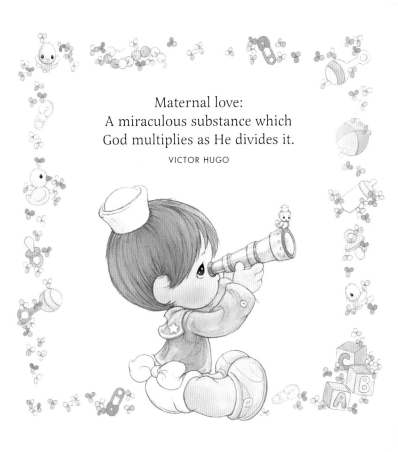

Maternal love:
A miraculous substance which
God multiplies as He divides it.

VICTOR HUGO

"Mother"—a word that means the world to me.

HOWARD JOHNSON

The future belongs to those who believe
in the beauty of their dreams.

ELEANOR ROOSEVELT

Blessed is the influence of one true,
loving human soul on another.

GEORGE ELIOT

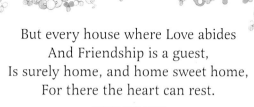

But every house where Love abides
And Friendship is a guest,
Is surely home, and home sweet home,
For there the heart can rest.

HENRY VAN DYKE

A mother is not a person; she's a miracle.

MARY HOLLINGSWORTH

A kind heart is a fountain of gladness,
making everything in its vicinity
freshen into smiles.

WASHINGTON IRVING

Happiness comes of the capacity to feel deeply,
to enjoy simply, to think freely, to risk life,
to be needed.

STORM JAMESON

If there be one thing pure...
that can endure,
when all else passes away...
it is a mother's love.

MARCHIONESS DE SPADARA